150.

Ber

11021

EARN YOUR ALLOWANCE

What to do when your mom or dad says . . .
"EARN YOUR ALLOWANCE!"

By

JOY WILT BERRY

Living Skills Press
Fallbrook, California

1

Distributed by:

Word, Incorporated
4800 W. Waco Drive
Waco, TX 76710

Dear Parents,

"EARN YOUR ALLOWANCE!" You've probably said that more than once to your child and received a less than enthusiastic response. Has it ever occurred to you that your child's resistance to your request may come from not knowing HOW to do what you have asked? Assuming that a child will automatically know how to fulfill a request is often the cause of much parent-child conflict.

If you expect your child to do something that he or she is not equipped to do, it is most likely that your child will become overwhelmed and anxious while you become frustrated. Both reactions are prime conditions for a knock-down-drag-out fight!

Why not avoid these kinds of encounters? Who needs them? Much of the negative "back and forth" that goes on between you and your child could be avoided if both of you approached your expectations intelligently.

Fulfilling **any** expectation always begins with knowing how. Skills are required to do any task, no matter what the task may be. These skills must be learned **before** the task can be accomplished. This is a fact of life!

All too often parents have left their children to discover these skills on their own through trial and error over a very long period of time. Why? You wouldn't give your child a complicated book in the beginning and say, "Teach yourself to read."

My suspicion is that most parents do not teach their children the skills they need to accomplish everyday tasks because they themselves do not know the skills and would therefore not know **what** to teach their child.

3

Does this apply to you? If it does, relax! "Earn Your Allowance" not only helps children, it helps parents survive as well.

If you will take the time to go through this book with your child, both of you will learn some **very** valuable skills ... skills that will really pay off in the long run.

Some children will be able to read the book and assimilate all of the information themselves, but in most cases, you'll get better, more long lasting, results if you use the "Show Me How Then Let Me Do It" method. Here's how it works:

Using this book as a guideline ...

1. Demonstrate how the task should be done by doing it yourself while your child watches.
2. Do the task together or encourage your child to do the task while you watch him. (Avoid criticizing and praise anything the child does correctly while you are watching.)
3. Let your child do the task alone.
4. Praise the work and express appreciation for what your child has done.

If you'll take a little bit of time to teach your child the skills needed to fulfill your requests, you'll save yourself a lot of energy in the long haul.

So don't just sit there ... do it ... and have fun while you're at it. Who knows, doing these nitty-gritty things with your child may give you some of the greatest experiences you'll ever have together ... surely some of the most rewarding.

Sincerely,

Joy Wilt Berry

Has your mother or father ever told you to ...

EARN YOUR ALLOWANCE!

Whenever your mom or dad tells you to earn your allowance do you wonder ...

If any of this sounds familiar to you, you're **going** to **love** this book!

Because it will tell you exactly how to determine what your allowance should be and how you can go about deserving it.

AN ALLOWANCE IS A SHARE OF THE FAMILY INCOME

As a member of your family, you are entitled to a share of your family's possessions (what your family owns). This means that in addition to food, clothing, and shelter, you should probably get a portion of any money that is made.

Yes, it is fantastic, but before you get too excited about sharing your family's possessions you need to consider the other side.

Belonging to any group requires an equal amount of **GIVE** and **TAKE.**

It is only fair that whenever you take something from a group you give something back to it. No one likes to be in a group with a person who is always taking and never giving in return. It just isn't fair! The same thing applies to your family. If you take something from your family, you must give something back to it.

PLENTY!

You can contribute to your family by **TAKING CARE OF YOURSELF.**

If you take care of yourself, no one else will have to do it for you, and this will be a big help! Help out by taking care of your own body. Keep it clean and well groomed every day.

Help out by making sure you have the right clothes to wear and by getting yourself dressed every day. You may need to plan what you are going to wear the night before you get dressed.

You can **take care of yourself** by preparing your own breakfast.

You can also help out by preparing your own lunch and snacks.

You can contribute to your family by **CLEANING UP AFTER YOURSELF.**

Help out by keeping your own bedroom organized and clean.

Help out by picking up and putting away **anything** you use in and around the house.

You can **clean up after yourself** by cleaning up **any mess** you make. This applies to "accidental" messes as well as ones made "on purpose."

You can also help out by doing things such as ...

— Flushing the toilet after you use it.

— Wiping off the toilet seat or floor around the toilet if you should accidentally "drip" on it.

— Turning out the lights in rooms you leave (if there is no one left in them).

— Turning water faucets completely off when you are finished using them.

Taking care of yourself and cleaning up after yourself will be a big help, but it is not enough. You need to give more than this, if you are to share your family's possessions.

You must decide along with your family what is a fair contribution for you to make. Listed below are a few jobs you may want to consider in coming up with your list of responsibilities.

- Set the table for meals.
- Clear the table after meals.
- If you do not have a dishwasher:
    wash the dishes
    dry the dishes (and put them away).
- If you have a dishwasher:
    load the dishwasher
    unload the dishwasher.
- Empty the trash.
- Take care of the family pets.
- Vacuum / sweep the floors.
- Sweep the outside porches and walks.
- Dust the furniture.
- Mow the lawn.
- Rake the leaves.
- Shovel the snow.

If you take care of yourself, clean up after yourself, and do the chores that your family asks you to do, you are entitled to an allowance.

How much allowance you receive is something that must be decided by your parents and you.

Several things need to be taken into consideration when deciding how much your allowance should be.

HOW MUCH MONEY YOUR FAMILY HAS

This is the most important thing to consider in deciding how much your allowance should be. A "fair" allowance is usually a percentage of the family's income.

The exact percentage must be up to you and your parents. Some families pay as much as ten percent of the net income, but most families pay around one percent. A "percentage" allowance works out better than a "fixed" one because the children share in the family's financial successes **and** setbacks.

Here is how a one percent allowance would work:

YOUR FAMILY'S INCOME (per year)	A one percent allowance would give you approximately		
	PER YEAR	PER MONTH	PER WEEK
$5,000.00	50.00	4.00	1.00
10,000.00	100.00	8.00	2.00
15,000.00	150.00	12.50	3.00
20,000.00	200.00	16.00	4.00
30,000.00	300.00	25.00	6.00
40,000.00	400.00	33.00	8.00
50,000.00	500.00	42.00	10.00

WHAT YOU ARE EXPECTED TO BUY

The more things which you are expected to pay for, the more money you should be given. Generally speaking, an allowance is expected to cover the following things:

— School supplies (the ones not provided by the school).
— Snacks (not provided by home or school).
— Entertainment (shows, bowling, skating, miniature golfing, etc.).
— Special equipment and supplies needed for hobbies or after-school activities.
— Special gifts to be given to another person (mom, dad, grandmother, best friend, etc.).
— Miscellaneous (any other items that are "nice" but not "necessary" for a child to have).

You and your parents may need to adjust either the amount of your allowance or the number of things you are expected to buy with it; otherwise it will only cause conflict between you and your parents.

HOW WELL YOU HANDLE MONEY

If you are irresponsible with your money, that is, if you spend all of it as fast as you get it on frivolous things that have no value, you should not be given very much money. It is important that you learn how to budget and spend money wisely before you are given very much of it.

HOW MUCH MONEY YOUR FRIENDS HAVE

Having more money than your friends causes just as many problems as having less than them. Both situations lead to feelings of jealousy, rejection, rivalry, and more. To avoid these problems, find out how much allowance your friends get and take this into consideration when deciding how much you should get.

Once your parents and you have decided what you are to do to earn your allowance and how much you are to be paid, it is time to follow through.

34

"Following through" with something is doing what you have decided to do. It is very important that both you and your parents follow through with the agreements you make with each other.

If you fail to take care of yourself, clean up after yourself, and/or do the chores that have been assigned to you, chances are someone else will have to do it for you. If and when this happens, it is only fair that the other person be paid for his or her services.

The other person will be paid with money subtracted from YOUR ALLOWANCE.

Here's how it works. With regard to taking care of yourself ...

If someone else has to do something you are to do for yourself, a certain amount of money will be subtracted from your allowance and paid to the person who helped you.

In regard to cleaning up after yourself ...

If someone else has to pick up or clean up after you, a certain amount of money will be subtracted from your allowance and paid to the person who did the work.

In regard to doing your chores ...

If you leave your chores for someone else to do, you should pay them with money subtracted from your allowance.

If at all possible you should receive your allowance ONCE A WEEK.

During the week you or your parents should fill in a chart that may look something like this:

TASK CHART

TASK	MON.	TUES.	WED.	THURS.	FRI.	SAT.	SUN.
Taking Care Of Yourself							
Took A Shower							
Brushed Teeth							
Got Dressed							
Combed Hair							
Made Breakfast							
Made Lunch							

TASK CHART Cont'd.

TASK	MON.	TUES.	WED.	THURS.	FRI.	SAT.	SUN.
Cleaning Up After Yourself							
Cleaned Bedroom							
Cleaned Up Any Mess Made							
Picked Up Own Things							
Miscellaneous							
Chores							
Set The Table							
Washed The Dishes							
Emptied The Trash							

Refer to the chart on pages 38 and 39. If you complete a task you or your parents should put a check in the appropriate square. If someone else did the task for you, his or her name should be written in the square instead of a check.

At the end of the week, all of the squares with another person's name in them are added up. The money necessary to pay for each square is then subtracted from your allowance and paid to the appropriate person. Penalties usually range from 10 cents to 50 cents, depending upon how much allowance is paid and how big or little the task is.

To encourage the people in your family to pick up after themselves, your family may want to do this.

At the end of each day have one person go around the house picking up everything that has been left out, and put the items in a large garbage bag.

As a penalty to the person who failed to pick up after himself or herself, the items should remain in the bag for one whole week and then be "purchased back" for 5 cents or 10 cents per item. This might encourage all family members to pick up after themselves.

To make sure your parents pay your allowance regularly and on time, you will need a second chart that may look something like this.

PAYMENT CHART

DATE	Allowance	Extra Earnings	Deductions	Amount Paid	Received By
5/7	3.00	.50		3.50	Heidi
5/14	3.00	1.25	.25	4.00	Heidi
5/21	3.00		1.00	2.00	Heidi

*Allowance + Extra Earnings - Deductions = Amount Paid

When you receive your weekly earnings, you must sign the chart. This is to show that you have been paid.

It is always nice to get things in writing, especially when money is involved. So to keep things clear and "up front" between you and your parents, it would be a good idea to have an allowance contract. The contract might look something like this.

I _____ on _____
 Your Name   Date

Agree to do the following:
Take care of myself by doing:

_____

_____

Clean up after myself by doing:

_____

_____

Do these following chores:

_____

_____

In exchange for these services, I am entitled to an allowance which is to be _____, to be paid _____ of every
        Amount of Allowance   Day
week.
My allowance is to cover all the following items: _____

____ _____

If I should fail to follow through with any of my responsibilities
_____ will be subtracted from my allowance and
   Amount

paid to the person who fulfilled my obligation.

If my allowance is not paid on the day agreed upon a penalty of
_____ will be paid for every day after the due date.
    Amount

Signed

_____   _____
Your signature   Date

_____   _____
Your parent's signature   Date

To make this system work it is extremely important that you **do not** ask your parents to give you money that you are not entitled to or that you do not earn. If your parents start **giving** you money, you will not respect it, and you will never learn how to use it wisely.

You can bargain with your parents to pay you for any **additional** tasks you do for the family. If they don't have any extra money, you'll have to get a job outside your home to supplement your allowance. Here is a list of some of the things you could do for your family to earn extra money:

— make and pack sack lunches for your family or fix other meals,
— clean and polish shoes,
— take care of the houseplants,
— clean and wax the furniture,
— take care of younger children (baby-sit),
— sew on buttons - mend clothing that needs fixing,
— polish metal household items (for example, silverware, brass knobs, etc.),
— clean and wash the car,
— weed the garden,
— wash the windows.

Whenever you do an extra job, be sure to write it down on your TASK CHART so that you will be sure to be paid for it.

THE END of arguments over your allowance!